Williaı at The ——— Hotel

CW00767797

Ten Newcastle Poets

Edited and introduced by
Paul Summers

'City lights don't shine, they glare
your music doesn't speak, it swears
And in your streets, the ghosts
have forgotten why they're there'

—Alan Hull

First published 2021 by **Culture Matters.**
Culture Matters promotes a socialist and progressive approach to art,
culture and politics.
See www.culturematters.org.uk

Text copyright © the contributors
Cover image © Crucible by Paul Summers
Other images © Dan Douglas
Edited by Paul Summers
Layout and typesetting by Alan Morrison
ISBN: 978-1-912710-23-2

*Thanks to UNISON Newcastle City branch and Newcastle Trades Union
Council for their support and sponsorship of this anthology.*

Foreword

By Martin Levy, President, Newcastle Trades Union Council

One of our aims on Newcastle Trades Union Council is to promote cultural opportunities for working people on Tyneside. We have a long history of involvement in culture, sponsoring and supporting many different kinds of cultural activities, including music, theatre, life-writing and visual art. We are also members of Newcastle's Culture Compact, a partnership of the City Council, cultural, health and educational agencies, which is developing a new strategy for cultural life in Newcastle over the next ten years.

We have concerns about various imbalances and injustices in the cultural life of Newcastle, which affect working people, particularly certain groups of working people including women, people of colour, and young people. Research has shown that there are deep, structural and long-lasting inequalities in the cultural landscape for these people. The inequalities are around their access as workers to secure, sustainable careers in the creative and cultural industries; their access as consumers to relevant, local, affordable cultural experiences; and the representation of their perspectives, characters and stories as working people in the cultural life of the city.

So we welcome and support this new anthology of poetry, rooted in the everyday experience of some of our finest creative writers. Sometimes this can mean 'singing in a powerless wasteland' as Keith Armstrong puts it; sometimes it is 'pigeons all turning into pigs that fly' as Joan Johnston writes; and sometimes this is 'just getting on with it', as Jane Burn puts it in one of her poems.

Always though, the poets are thoroughly engaged with local history and with current social and political issues, and authentically reflecting many of the problems and difficult situations as well as the joys and satisfactions of working people on Tyneside.

We intend to make this book available as a printed book and as an ebook to all the unions affiliated to the Trades Council, so that they in turn can circulate it to the 40,000 or so trade union members in the city. We will seek feedback on this exercise, and intend to support future creative projects of socially engaged cultural production by local working people.

i

Introduction

By Paul Summers

ewcastle, like most cities, has never been short of poetic representations. rom the popular gin-house Victorian bards and songsmiths to the more cademic and 'bourgeois' chroniclers of the latter half of the twentieth entury and the early decades of this one, there exist many poetic insights ito this city and its inhabitants. Between the two, there lies a whole body f works written by working-class poets that remains largely marginalised, ivisible and 'unpopular'. 'Unpopular' not because of their poetic worth, ut limited largely by contemporary poetry's cultural reach, the limits of ie independent presses and magazines to extend into new 'markets', id the limited number of genuinely popular vehicles of transmission, as ell as by the changing nature of the general public's consumption of all iings poetic.

his collection presents ten writers who are diverse in style but unified / generation, politics and class. As such, their visions of the city and its ople represent a very particular and interesting socio-cultural moment. is a moment which straddles an epoch of archetypal working-class mmunities and their subsequent dismantling, a time of transition from dustry and post-industry, perhaps even a transition from lumpen and ten romantic representations of the north east to a more nuanced and mplex reality. It makes no claims to speak for, or to, everyone; but it's iportant that voices like these, the city's intimate reporters, are given an ring and their validity within a Novocastrian cultural canon reiterated.

ie accompanying photographs by Dan Douglas complement and expand i the texts. His images combine abstraction with concrete representation, oking oblique, non-traditional perspectives rather than the cliched idges and Georgian mercantile grandeur of the city centre, finding ternative layers of beauty and interest.

iere undoubtedly needs to be regular follow-ups to an anthology :e this, and hopefully organisations like the Trades Council, individual ide unions and **Culture Matters** will be able to facilitate this through a ogramme of socially engaged community arts projects. There needs to a growing library of ordinary people representing themselves rather an being perpetually represented by others. It needs to be a library with contributions garnered from a broader communion of commentators and observers with a much wider generational representation, with contributions from emergent voices from the city's culturally diverse communities, from the workplace and the broader community rather than just from the garrets of those of us who are already culturally and creatively active.

If an initiative like this is properly supported—a big 'if' in this climate of austerity and plague—this model can be rolled out in every city and town in the north east, collating not just poems by working-class people but fiction, drama, visual art and music. Only then might we begin to create a cultural landscape for our localities and experiences that looks even remotely democratic.

Contents

Keith Armstrong

'I was born in Heaton. My father was a shipyard worker, my mother a nurse. After leaving school, I qualified as a librarian but have spent the majority of my working (and now supposedly retired) life as a community arts worker, itinerant poet, literature promoter, instigator of community publishing initiatives and international twinning projects. The rationale behind most of this activity has been to give a platform to working-class experiences and voices to be seen and heard in a wider audience.'

I Will Sing Of My Own Newcastle

sing of my home city
sing of a true geordie heart
sing of a river swell in me
sing of a sea of the canny
sing of the newcastle day

sing of a history of poetry
sing of the pudding chare rain
sing of the puddles and clarts
sing of the bodies of sailors
sing of the golden sea

sing of our children's' laughter
sing of the boats in our eyes
sing of the bridges in sunshine
sing of the fish in the tyne
sing of the lost yards and the pits

sing of the high level railway
sing of the love in my face
sing of the garths and the castle
sing of the screaming lasses
sing of the sad on the side

sing of the battles' remains
sing of the walls round our dreams
sing of the scribblers and dribblers
sing of the scratchers of livings
sing of the quayside night

sing of the kicks and the kisses
sing of the strays and the chancers
sing of the swiggers of ale

sing of the hammer of memory
sing of the welders' revenge

sing of a battered townscape
sing of a song underground
sing of a powerless wasteland
sing of a buried bard
sing of the bones of tom spence

sing of the cocky bastards
sing of a black and white tide
sing of the ferry boat leaving
sing of cathedral bells crying
sing of the tyneside skies

sing of my mother and father
sing of my sister's kindness
sing of the hope in my stride
sing of a people's passion
sing of the strength of the wind

The Sun On Danby Gardens

The sun on Danby Gardens
smells of roast beef,
tastes of my youth.
The flying cinders of a steam train
spark in my dreams.
Across the old field,
a miner breaks his back
and lovers roll in the ditches,
off beaten tracks.

Off Bigges Main,
my grandad taps his stick,
reaches for the braille of long-dead strikes.
The nights
fair draw in
and I recall Joyce Esthella Antoinette Giles
and her legs that reached for miles,
tripping over the stiles
in red high heels.
It was her and blonde Annie Walker
who took me in the stacks
and taught me how to read
the signs
that led inside their thighs.
Those Ravenswood girls
would dance into your life
and dance though all the snow drops
of those freezing winters,
in the playground of young scars.
And I remember freckled Pete
who taught me Jazz,
who pointed me to Charlie Parker
and the edgy bitterness of Brown Ale.
Mrs Todd next door
was forever sweeping
leaves along the garden path
her fallen husband loved to tread.
Such days:
the smoke of A4 Pacifics in the aftermath of war,
the trail of local history on the birthmarked street.
And I have loved you all my life
and will no doubt die in Danby Gardens
where all my poems were born,
just after midnight.

The Streets Of Tyne

I kicked out in Half Moon Yard,
bucked a rotten system.
Fell out with fools in All Hallows Lane
and grew up feeling loved.

She dragged my hand down Rabbit Banks Road,
there seemed nowhere else to take it.
We mucked about in Plummer Chare,
soaked up the painful rain.

I wanted to control my life,
shout songs on Amen Corner.
I'd carry bags of modern ballads,
hawk pamphlets on Dog Bank.

Wild girls who blazed through Pipewell Gate
taught my veins to thrill.
I caught her heart on Pandon Bank,
my eyes filled up with fear.
Wanted to carve out a poem,
inspire the Garth Heads dreamers.
A lad grew up to dance along
the length of Pilgrim Street.

I take my wild hopes now to chance
the slope of Dog Leap Stairs.
Follow the pulse of my Tyneside days,
burn passion down The Side.

Splinters
(*For My Father*)

You picked splinters
with a pin each day
from under blackened fingernails;
shreds of metal
from the shipyard grime,
minute memories of days swept by:
the dusty remnants of a life
spent in the shadow of the sea;
the tears in your shattered eyes
at the end of work.
And your hands were strong,
so sensitive and capable
of building boats
and nursing roses;
a kind and gentle man
who never hurt a soul,
the sort of quiet knackered man
who built a nation.
Dad, I watched your ashes float away
down to the ocean bed
and in each splinter
I saw your caring eyes
and gracious smile.

I think of your strong silence every day
and I am full of you,
the waves you scaled,
and all the sleeping Tyneside streets
you taught me to dance my fleeting feet along.

When I fly, you are with me.
I see your fine face
in sun-kissed clouds
and in the gold ring on my finger,
and in the heaving crowd on Saturday,
and in the lung of Grainger Market,
and in the ancient breath
of our own Newcastle.

Heaton Junction

This is where I was joined to the world,
this is where I first appeared
and took to walking
along the sun-baked pavements
on the route of the 15 bus.
I joined
with the Heaton race,
found a sense of place
out of my mother's arms
and up Sackville Road
to Ravenswood.
Junctions rushed towards me,
engines of progress,
steam days in the 52B shed.
Magical machines
flew past me
along the quarter mile sidings
in the coaly night
as the local cats screamed
and young dogs yelped.
It was my time

to run with my youth
and someone threw me
a book to disappear in,
something to engage
my history with,
streets lining up
for exploration;
feeding off
Chillingham Road,
getting lost
in the Scala,
eyes swirling
with street life,
the Whitefield Terrace colours
of another teeming Heaton day.
There I was
chucking snowballs
at trains,
skimming along rails,
falling
for girls on the ice.
We pranced together,
joined gangs of trees
in the Park,
threw ourselves
into the smoke from chimneys,
dreamed through the nights
of black locomotives,
joining us to London
and Edinburgh,
taking us out
of ourselves.
We don't forget
those junctions
that linked us

to the wealth
of a history shimmering
in the back lanes
and in the leaves
dancing in sunlight
in Jesmond Dene,
running across Armstrong Bridge
to greet
our futures.

Angels Playing Football

Some weeks before he died in 1988, the legendary Newcastle United footballer Jackie Milburn was sitting in his Ashington home with a granddaughter on his knee. Outside, there was thunder and lightning, which frightened the wee girl: 'What's that noise?', she asked her grandad anxiously. 'Don't worry', 'Wor Jackie' replied, 'It's just the angels playing football.' It was this incident which inspired the following poem, given added poignancy by the placing of an Alan Shearer shirt on the Gateshead Angel's prodigious back by local fans before the 1998 F.A. Cup Final!

Sprinkle my ashes on St. James's Park,
Fragments of goals on the grass.
Hear the Gallowgate roar in the dark.
All of my dreams came to pass.

Pass me my memories,
Pass me the days,
Pass me a ball and I'll play:

Play with the angels,
Play on their wings,
Play in the thunder and lightning.

I leave you these goals in my will,
Snapshots of me on the run.
I leave you these pieces of skill,
Moments of me in the sun.

Pass me my memories,
Pass me the days,
Pass me a ball and I'll play:

Play with the angels,
Play on their wings,
Play in the thunder and lightning.

Folk Song For Thomas Spence
(1750-1814)

Down by the old Quayside,
I heard a young man cry,
among the nets and ships he made his way.
As the keelboats buzzed along,
he sang a seagull's song;
he cried out for the Rights of you and me.

Oh lads, that man was Thomas Spence,
he gave up all his life
just to be free.
Up and down the cobbled Side,
struggling on through the Broad Chare,
he shouted out his wares
for you and me.

Oh lads, you should have seen him gan,
he was a man the likes you rarely see.
With a pamphlet in his hand,
and a poem at his command,
he haunts the Quayside still
and his words sing.

His folks they both were Scots,
sold socks and fishing nets,
through the Fog on the Tyne they plied their trade.
In this theatre of life,
the crying and the strife,
they tried to be decent and be strong.

Oh lads, that man was Thomas Spence,
he gave up all his life
just to be free.
Up and down the cobbled Side,
struggling on through the Broad Chare,
he shouted out his wares
for you and me.

Oh lads, you should have seen him gan,
he was a man the likes you rarely see.
With a pamphlet in his hand,
and a poem at his command,
he haunts the Quayside still
and his words sing.

(from the music-theatre piece 'Pig's Meat' written for Bruvvers Theatre Company)

Walk On, Tom Bewick

Stride Circus Lane
and chip your signature
on the pavement of scrapes and kisses.
Pass the Forth
and skirt
its pleasure gardens;
throw your darts in the archery field.
Skim the bowling green
and walk on water,
doff your hat to Mrs Waldie;
cut along
old scars of lanes
to the bloody gush of Westgate Street;
whistle with birds
in a vicar's garden,
let warm thoughts fly in Tyneside sun
to bless this Geordie day.
And greet
the morning hours,
Aunt Blackett and Gilbert Gray,
sing to free the world,
the Black Boy;
harmonise your mind
in a churchyard of melancholy.
Dance over the Lort Burn,
the sun in your eyes,
flooding your workshop
with a light fantastic.
Your shoulders so proud
rub with the building girls
and lady barbers
along Sandhill;
the boats of your dreams

bridge the aching Tyne,
ships groaning
in the tender daylight,
longing for the healing moon;
a keelman's fantasies
of quayside flesh
and the seething sea.
You trip along
searching for electricity and magnetism
in the inns,
winging it
with the bird catchers and canary breeders,
the dirty colliers and the harping whalers.
Walk on Tom,
execute
a portrait
of a hanging man;
let your strong heart
swell with the complex passion
of common folk.

For 'Cuny'

'Search where Ambition rag'd, with rigour steel'd;
Where Slaughter, like the rapid lightning, ran;
And say, while mem'ry weeps the blood-stain'd field,
Where lies the chief, and where the common man?'

(John Cunningham)

'Unto thy dust, sweet Bard! adieu!
Thy hallow'd shrine I slowly leave;
Yet oft, at eve, shall Mem'ry view
The sun-beam ling'ring on thy grave.'

(David Carey)

This week an elegant tombstone, executed by Mr. Drummond of this town,
was set up in St. John's church-yard to the memory of the late ingenious Mr.
John Cunningham. The following is the inscription thereon:

'Here lie the Remains of JOHN CUNNINGHAM.
Of his Excellence as a Pastoral Poet,
His Works will remain a Monument
For Ages
After this temporary Tribute of Esteem
Is in Dust forgotten.
He died in Newcastle, Sept 18, 1773,
Aged 44.'

The ritual slaughter
of traffic,
hurling itself
against the furious economy,
the commerce of suffering,
the pain of money,
nudges your bones
in this graveyard of hollow words.
I hear you liked a jar
well, here's me

sprinkling
your precious monument
with a little local wine,
lubricating the flowers
that burst from your pastoral verses.

You toured the boards like me,
torn like me,
with your heart,
terrific heart,
pouring real blood on your travelling sleeve.
Oh, my God!
your lips trembled
with a delicate love
for the fleeting joy,
the melancholic haze,
the love in a mist,
that Tom Bewick sketched in you
amd Mrs Slack fed
as you passed along
this way and that
despair in your eyes.
The fact was
you were not born
for the rat race
of letters,
the ducking and fawning
for tasteless prizes,
the empty bloated rivalry,
the thrust of their bearded egos.
You wanted wonder,
the precise touch
of the sun on your grave,
the delicious kiss
that never comes back.

I'm with you, 'Cuny'
in this Newcastle Company of Comedians;
I'm in your clouds of drunken ways;
I twitch with you
in my poetic nervousness
along Westgate Road.
And the girls left their petals for you
like I hope they do for me
in the light of the silver moon,
thinking of your pen
scratching stars into the dark sky.

Byker Hill
(Published by IRD Arts Club 1972)

byker

antique mart of memory's remnants

glad bag of fading rags

bedraggled old flag

blowing in the wind over newcastle

we stand on street corners shivering in the winter
like birds sheltering from the wind

we do not rattle loose change in our pockets
only the nuts and bolts of poverty
we are splinters

ill-shaven
our clothes droop on us
using our bones for hangers

we avoid mirrors and images of ourselves in shields road doorways
we do not look through windows

we draw curtains of beer across our eyes
we sleep/place bets

every week on dole day hunger prods us awake

it is instinct

it is a fear of never waking

yesterday's records in a raby street window
yesterday's news
revolving today

pictures of byker trapped in a camera
yesterday's photos
developed today

yesterday's headlines
today's wrapping paper

yesterday's wars are bloodless today

snot drips nose
wailing ragman drags a foot
and sniffs

any old rags
any old rags

hair like straw
homespun
snot runs
licks cracked mouth

any old rags
any old rags

as raby street
  declines
          into
water

any old rags
any old rags

watson's toffee factory
wrapped in mist
melts in the watering mouth of the dawn
another byker child is born

another byker son assumes
the dusty jacket of a byker man

and this is the truth
the wind-ripped reality between the grave and the womb
the aimlessness

the weary broken people
shuffling through the measured lines of architects' reports

the cripples
the dying streets
behind the brash and snatching shops
the coughing strays

this is all the *small* print
the drifting words
beneath the glossy covers

and this is mother byker now

a wasteland of schools
churches public houses
a frail old woman
her mouth and eyes bricked over
tilting

on her last legs

change
creeps like a lizard over the face of byker
dragging behind it it's retinue of planners
    wreckers
    builders and
    visionaries

tomorrow
you will wake from your years of sleeping
and find what you knew to be yours being hauled away
over byker bridge on the backs of lorries
your yesterday

in clouds of dust

byker folk are living still
byker folk on byker hill
fading flowers on a window sill
byker folk
　　hang
　on

William Blake In The Bridge Hotel

A few pints of Deuchars and my spirit is soaring.
The child dances out of me,
goes running down to the Tyne,
while the little man in me wrestles with a lass
and William Blake beams all his innocence in my glass.
And the old experience sweats from a castle's bricks
as another local prophet takes a jump off the bridge.

It's the spirit of Pat Foley and the ancient brigade
on the loose down the Quayside stairs
in a futile search,
just a step in the past,
for one last revolutionary song.

All the jars we have supped
in the hope of a change;
all the flirting and courting and chancing downstream;
all the words in the air and the luck pissed away.
It seems we oldies are running back
screaming to the Bewick days,

when a man could down a politicised quip
and craft a civilised chat
before he fed the birds
in the Churchyard.

The cultural ships are fair steaming in
but it's all stripped of meaning—
the Councillors wade
in the shallow end.

O Blake! buy me a pint in the Bridge again,
let it shiver with sunlight
through all the stained windows,
make my wit sparkle
and my knees buckle.

Set me free of this stifling age
when the bland are back in charge.
Let us grow our golden hair wild once more
and roar like Tygers
down Dog Leap Stairs.

An Oubliette For Kitty

There's a hole in this Newcastle welcome,
there's a beggar with a broken spine.
On Gallowgate, a heart is broken
and the ships have left the Tyne.

So what becomes of this History of Pain?
What is there left to hear?
The kids pour down the Pudding Chare lane
and drown a folksong in beer.

So here is an oubliette for you, Kitty,
somewhere to hide your face.
The blood is streaming from fresh wounds in our city
and old scars are all over the place.

There's this dirt from a history of darkness
and they've decked it in neon and glitz.
There are traders in penthouse apartments
on the Quayside where sailors once pissed.

So where are Hughie and Tommy, Kitty?,
the ghosts of Geordies past?
I don't want to drown you in pity
but I saw someone fall from the past.

So here is an oubliette for you, Kitty,
somewhere to hide your face.
The blood is streaming from fresh wounds in our city
and old scars are all over the place.

While they bomb the bridges of Belgrade,
they hand us a cluster of Culture
and tame Councillors flock in on a long cavalcade
to tug open the next civic sculpture.

And who can teach you a heritage?
Who can learn you a poem?
We're lost in a difficult, frightening, age
and no one can find what was home.

So here is an oubliette for you, Kitty,
somewhere to hide your face.
The blood is streaming from fresh wounds in our city
and old scars are all over the place.

So here is an oubliette for you, Kitty,
somewhere to hide your face.
The blood is streaming from fresh wounds in our city
and old scars are all over the place.

Jane Burn

'What does it mean to be a working-class voice? That is a long and difficult question. I was asked at a poetry reading recently about the effect alienation has had on my poetry. I guess that is a long and difficult question too, but my answer did include how alienation is intrinsically part of working-class life.

I grew up knowing that there were so many things I would never be—imagine your life so limited, before you have even lived it! Perhaps a better way to put it would be to say there were so many things I didn't know I could be. What is that word again? That one we are called when we tell it how it is? When we express our anger at the inequality of our lives? That's right. Chippy. We're nothing but resentful, after all. It is very easy to dismiss working-class anger as only a matter of this.

The way we have had to fight so much harder to be where we are now, and spend our whole lives balanced upon the edge of a knife, makes us the writers and artists we are. To have spent our decades surrounded by poverty, poor education, unemployment, strikes, the death of industries, unhappiness, violence and the rest of society's distorted view of who we are is bound to influence what comes from our hearts, our heads and the end of our pens.'

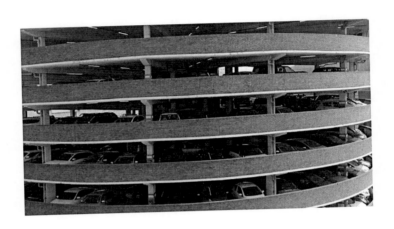

Under the Bells

Inspired by Newcastle Cathedral and a walk to Central Station

The plangent rail of metal rings—clappers proudly mistimed,
asking worshippers to *come!* Pray to the hour of Evensong,
sound calling down in a holy wheel of noise. Come!
How it has my heartstrings! *Here is your God! This
is your Tower Of Faith!* Lit with gold against the fall of night,
I feel I'm under a wonder of the world though 'tis only mingled bells.
A couple, paused in rain—she's looking up at him, all kohl and lips,
like she's looking at Jesus. I see the hasp of his bicep flex,
feel the cold-wet in my toes. It's winter though I still wear
my peep-toed shoes and fuchsia socks. I have no fear of gaudy feet—
I hear the bells calling *heaven decries your fashion, see it weep.*
I fear I'll lose the wedding sound in the slap of tyres on tarmac,
hiss of bus brakes, static tannoy barking through the station's arches
but still the ding-dong-merrily escapes, crystal past the chug
of diesel taxis – across the ripples of kinky pavements, puddles
the shape of fallen pain. People rushing, some with ears plugged
into bubbles of song—seems there are a million, million bodies,
some with woolly hats or suits or gloves. Lady with honey hair
shoulders a Boss tote—someone near me smells of chips.
Passing car windows are slick with heat and exhaled breath. I see a child
make her mark in condensation—finger squiggles make me think
of everyone I love or have loved. Trees festoon with rats of plastic bag—
take-out packets smother the wet in paper cloaks and crowds stride
quick upon them. I look for an angel in everyone—some face
in a passing car turns bright in circle to me, smiles. Bloke outside
the boozer raises up an arm, proud as an Elasmotherium's
prong, does a bit of shouting, howls a snatch of a *Toon Army* chant.
Yellow light makes crowns upon the road, anoints the crowd,
coronates our common heads. The bells have faded to tin whispers.
It's humans make the rabble now, not campanology—
tongues now preach carillons while getting pissed.
Tonsils are bourdons, echoing throats with octaves of nonsense.
Their chimes are severed by the station's automatic doors.

Wave at Aeroplanes
Inspired by a supermarket in Blaydon

Lady on an escalator, pudging her phone screen as if probing apples
for spots—I want to shrill *look up! The skylights are squares of heaven!*
I am dazzled by haloes, falling as irritation on text, as they fall
in blessings on my head. *Look up!* The auto-stairway swaps us, one up,
one down—there is nothing I can do for her frowns save lift my arms,
madwoman on a metal slide, sponging the last of the sun. *Look!*

To top shelves in supermarkets, where the weird things are—discover
arrowroot, boxes of Trill. *Health for your budgerigar.* Budgerigar!
Such a word for a small, blue-green bird! A word as big as Apocalypse—
so much more than feathers! I picture frailest shells of beak cracking on
droplets of spherical seed. Kissing their bell-rung mirrors, hanging from
nails in summer—cuttlefish biters, watching the free. *Look up!*

I look for broken lovers. Don't come to me if you are brand new—
I will dirty you. Eyes with blossoms of marigold agony, you and me,
we can grow gardens of disaster. *Look up!* Together we can be lifeboats,
we can be umbrellas. Come to my arms—I will not be afraid! *Look up!*
Wonder where the dead are, missing from your cosset—some days
if you could only touch them one more time! The Gone do not return

except in backs of minds—they have already found their truth and lie
in peace while mourners line the hole like jars of wails. *Hold them
while they are alive! Look up!* See dizzy bumbles pissed on pollen,
wave at aeroplanes taking everyone to and from. Wait for constellations.
Make Pyxis or Columba—*pretend you know where they are!* Nod sagely
at satellites. *Look up!* Dandelion clocks and carrier bags! We do not need

this study of pavements—counting the cracks is somebody else's job.

It's Snowing, Sally

Where are you? It's cold—skimmer on the draggled bushes,
west of where you were last seen. I am one inch shorter than you.
Putting my feet where you put yours, I leave a clear tale in the crisp.

Are you there? The smell of ruined damp, the feel of the safety rail
under the weight of my ribs. It would take no effort to tip.
The rivergall closes a hush over what it keeps—does it have you,

snagged in the tumblewood, or crooked in the stilts of the staiths?
When the tide goes out, shapes guess themselves beneath the clag.
Once, teemers and trimmers dropped the noise of their voices

into the dun filth. Are your last sounds left to the mud?
Was your dirige slicked on the rainbow oil? The colours seem
as if they are holding song. Pooled in my bath back home,

I am pretending to be you. The wound in the bathwater left
by my sousing head heals quickly. I wish I was not so fat and big
in this tub then I could ebb, loosely bump on the plastic banks.

I open my mouth—it fills with the taste of tepid skin, soap scum, self.
The Tyne would taste of ruined world, engine spill, iron. To remain
on the bottom too long would mean being folded into silt.

The Swing Bridge lies its swiveled arc on a pier of timber traps.
A monster's creel, a bewilderment of sodden stilts. Maybe I see
a pale shuttle, washed in the loom of its legs. There is no affirmation

that you fell, nor hurtled, nor lurched. I have gotten to thinking of you
as a mermaid. You are not beached somewhere, tangled with tide lines,
nor caught in the keel of the Brekaer, coffin as she is. You could have

gone out to sea—could have been taken by the ebb. I walked
all the way to the Lemington Gut—there is old timber where
the iron works used to be. I did not find you there.

Are You Still Walking?
On searching the Quayside and up to Shields Road

Follow the Quayside from that hotel, the one where you walked
through lamp-spill. See the automated smile of the Swing,
Pass beneath the green icon of the Tyne, see the pared arc

of the Millenium. Do not shudder—bridges are not out to get you.
Walk one, tipsy with thoughts of the drop, career
to the unnatural view of water, dozens of feet below. Walk it back,

to let it know it cannot claim you. Keep going, past where everything
is spanking new. Go left at Ouse Street, take Byker Bank—discover
that you have made it as far as Shields Road. Wor Jackie's is gone,

ages now but the Raby is still packed with folk, pissed as farts
by noon. Smell the baking pasties—eat one as you go
from the paper bag, golden flakes about you, marking your path

like Hansel's crumbs. Look through the window of the *Singing Hinny*,
made nebulous by tea-stoked breath, search the faces, marbled by fug.
A tongue chases a bleed of yolk, some kid drops a scree of bits.

Open the door and wear the glancing of barely curious eyes.
Make yourself ready to say *hello*. Take off your coat.
Be baffled that you don't see her, sitting there.

Skinnerburn Road

Part I

In January, the rain did not stop
for three days—biblical, almost.
Everywhere sluicing wet, down, down,
down, searching for somewhere to pool.
To collect, accrete to burn, river, sea.
So much wet that it took the wall away.
On the twelfth day of your vanishment,
wall and land gave up its hold and spilled,
came this close to wiping away the lofts.

Today, eighty four days since you left,
I park my car near the fascination of crees.
The defiance of this hillside shanty—pallets,
buckshee junk, bottle-gas stoves, stained cups,
sacked seed. The trellised crenellations and
bright painted bits a *fuck you* to the smartening
of the Quayside. Skinnerburn Road is something
that cannot be cured with polish. I wonder if
you looked to them as you passed, as I cannot

resist doing. They tow your gaze, stare back,
paused like the birds they house, waiting for flight.
Through their chicken-wired eyes they saw you,
alive in the dawn from their parlous town,
their scrapyard eyrie, piggledy outlines pricking
the first hours of new day. Four hundred hearts,
bloom and ash, burned to death in the fire of 2014.
You and all the other ghosts of the river—
I can sense the scars you have left in the air.

Skinnerburn Road

Part 2

So different in the bright of day, this smut and ruin,
old-industrial, un-killable remnant of another time.
A time that won't catch up to the way things are meant
to be now, it is a tenacious blight, a stubborn argonaut,
suckers latched to the prettified town. A marker for where
the smart can end and the slipping back into memory
can begin. At night, a change settles on the long, straight road.
A smell of stilled dank from the quiet river, moonlight
on the underside of the Redheugh Bridge. Down
Shot Factory Lane, I see a group come out of the scrub,
where people go to shoot-up, drink, get out of their brains.
I look at them. They see me and their shouts are wolf-kill.
Run. There is a voice at my ear. *Run!* She says. Sally,
I see your shadow at the very corner of my right eye.
we run together—she cannot quite keep pace with me,
my pumps, slap-quick-slap, hers silent. If folk knew
what I think, what I believe they would sidelong glance me,
move a little further away. I reach my car, fumble the door,
get in, snap down the lock. You take the back seat.
We have a slow drive past the Business Park, along the water,
to absorb the resting skeleton of the Staiths. I leave you
at the traffic lights, turn left onto Scotswood Road,
for you must ever remain within the Tyne's ken.

Thistlecrack
Dedicated to Living in Wallsend

Telephones are malevolent. Cradle-bones biding
until you have felt the evening's quietness spread
above the room and you, uneasy, try to settle below it.

Then, it will rack the air with shrill—you leap
from the chair, stub a toe in your hurry to answer. It slips,
soapy from your hands. This is how the complexities

of twilight pass. Dusk is easy to close the curtains against—
night comes like the healing of a wound. You close your door
upon it, shove the key down the throat of the lock, spin it dead.

Dawns keep coming—it has been your habit to rise to them.
Mornings you squat on the step, watching sun fledge
through the wall's topping of broken glass, edges tinkered

with glim. You know how jagged this place is. How it makes you
afraid. Policemen knock in a way peculiar to them—
their knuckles on wood say *something's wrong* and you heart

is all clatterbash in your chest. Tonight, they are door-to-door
after someone called about screams on nearby scrub. You say,
it's vixens make a noise like that but even as they go, slicing

the wasteland with knives of light, coining a fox's eyes with beams,
you lie in bed, headful of murder grasses and think how a pair
of arms would be a comfort. You live where you can afford to live—

most days, you just get on with it and dream of fields. Exist in
little things—see how fingers of spruce grasp invisible wind, how,
in a thistlecrack, petals feather from spiny bulbs, turn to down.

Step to avoid torched bins. When you live somewhere rough,
you can choose to hold sun in your eyes. Search out the trees.
Discover the best and worst of places look beautiful under snow.

Sally, I seek you after a difficult day

On Scotswood Bridge at dusk, I watch the pink of sky,
clouds carried on the skin of the Tyne. I could be anyone—
hair bunched in a band, cardigan, scarf. Every few seconds,
a green light flashes from the old railway bridge. I lean
on the thick metal sides, though my knees shake
at the thought of the drop—I am afraid of being up so high,
yet tempted to cross by the fading world below.
I have been working on changing my life—have lost
a little weight, am becoming conscious of bones beneath.
This night, this mute, windless time is birdless, desolate,
beautiful. Stiff with fear upon the span, I can feel
its rock-a-bye movements—I pin my soles firmly down,
ride the wave of vertigo, swallow a scream. I think
this is a perfect night for haunting—Sally,
this is a perfect night for you.

Nev Clay

'I ran creative writing and song writing groups in prisons and mental hospitals, in local community groups and at the Sage Gateshead, for a decade. It's amazing to hear someone read (or sing)their own work for the first time. I remember a pensioner from Low Fell who wrote a song about Saltwell Park, and can still hear the chorus in my head. We performed it in the big hall with full choir and backing band, him in the front row, tears in his eyes.

Though I'd written poems since I was a kid, I'd never read aloud, or heard others read, until I started going to Newcastle-based groups like Stand and Deliver, the Blue Room, Diamond Twig events, the Morden Tower and the Billy Liar creative writing classes in the 90s. Stand and Deliver (and, later, Dharma Banana) was that rare sort of night where anyone could turn up, put their name down on the list, and read in front of their peers. Once a year, Graham Brown (who ran Stand and Deliver) would put out a little anthology including as many people who'd read as possible. First time I'd seen one of my poems printed.

I miss those nights, I learned so much, and they spurred me on to write more. It's struck me during the lockdown that, though there's been plenty online opportunities to be a spectator, to watch and listen, those ad hoc chances I got in upstairs pubs don't seem to exist online. It'd be helpful, I think, if they did.'

Bus

The empty pop bottle bounces down the stairs
The empty pop bottle rolls up the aisle
The empty pop bottle rolls across the aisle
The empty pop bottle rolls down the aisle

At the stop past the roundabout
The bottle rolls down the front
Someone kicks it off
And calm is restored

Home

Harry over the hallway
was a merchant seaman
Now, red ears and hands
he collects glasses for free beer
down the Social, the stairwell warm
with the smell of Scotch for
minutes after his return

6am some mornings
he throws out white bread
for the birds then yells
Go on, you little twats
Afternoons off
he swears at Westerns and Musicals

The morning after he threw a kitchen chair
through his living-room window
I heard him shout
clear as day:
Hold my hand

Lines

at the pond by the staff creche
a heron presides over
frog-hatching day

the college kid with KORN
written on his haversack
gets a warning for being
two minutes late
three times in three months
later, there's a cabbage white
in the plexiglass smoking bubble

the sixth form girl
who likes to wear red
is getting sacked tonight
for having tonsilitis
no tomato soup left
in the vending machine

as I pass with a
plastic cup of latte
the Asian lad from Sunderland
is saying again
No sir, this isn't Bombay

the sixteen year old
who already knows the difference
between reactive and
endogenous depression
leaves today for a
job at Orange
I bought a broccoli quiche
at Iceland for her

goodbye party
the girl who asks me if
I'm going for one last tab
sits reading her text messages
while I look at her stars
in the free paper

Pizza Crunch

We're in his flat in the Byker Wall
south-facing
he's holding the bairn
softly in his arms
singing her Smiths songs but
changing the words
like "miserable now" to "happy now"
and using her name

He tells me him, the bairn and the mam
are heading up the road to Coatbridge
to visit the family
Last time he was there, he says
he saw it in a chippy:
battered, deep-fried pizza
does the accent
"giza pizza crunch
ana puddin supper for the wee'en"

The winter light bounces off the river
off the sky and the city
somehow, passing through double-glazing
it becomes warm, golden
nourishing

The new neighbours

After an industrious weekend
clearing a year's grass and weeds
the new neighbours put up
an optimistic dovecote

On Summer nights
pipistrelles loop silently
above the little white house

Looney Tunes

Is what they call
the bloke at the front of the bus
when they get on laughing
at the stop by the Bingo

He must be fifty, glasses
thick as telescope lenses
white hair, jogging gear
and an ex-driver's belly

He hangs onto the handrails on corners
At the junction by the church
says to the driver "It's right here, mate"
The driver says "cheers, mate"
turning right

Into the estate, and he's
leaning back against the folding doors
I wait for him to move
As I squeeze past, he says unprompted
"It's since me mam died last year"

St.John's, Westgate Road

Who buried the men who
buried the men who buried
these Georgian industrialists
and their sickly families?
Where are the graves of the
gravediggers?

Behind a privet hedge
against the back wall of the church
an abandoned triangular road sign
that slightly comical silhouette:
the bent figure
the shaft of a shovel and
a pile of earth

Community 1

There's only the three of us
in the tinselled paper shop
a specky kid behind the till
the big lass filling shelves with crisps
and me, still wet with snow.
It's dark outside. On the radio
Paul Simon's "You can call me Al"
Comes on, and we all start dancing
In a quiet, happy way

Bus III

When I get on the bus
something is wrong—
everyone's smiling
Centre stage, near the front
a little red-headed kid
is standing on her Mam's plump legs
and singing

The bus driver is smiling too
He turns back and shouts
through the plastic partition
"There's only one thing wrong with that bairn
—when she grows up, she'll be a woman"
Only the singing kid
doesn't feel the temperature
change from Celsius
to Fahrenheit

Cuddy's Cave

From Yeavering Bell to Meadow Well
Cambois sands to *Poundland*
Bus stops, vape shops
Babies in black and white tops
Keegan's perm, the Lambton Worm
Standing stones, payday loans
Watch for traffic calming zones
On the green belt, starter homes
On the green belt, starter homes

From Wallington Hall to the Byker Wall
Kielder skies, meat pies
The Dyke Neuk, *Barter Books*,
Peter Barratts, organic carrots
Beardsley's face, the Blaydon Race
Tab breaks, stottie cakes
Doggerland to Matalan
Tynemouth pier, Gazza's tears
Tynemouth pier, Gazza's tears

Open cast, mobile masts
Bolam Lake, Crispy Pancakes
Greggs Steak Bakes, I, Daniel Blake
Caravan sites, pigeon shite
Tyres round the streetlights
Saxon monks, the smell of skunk
Landfill, roadkill,
my affection for little blue pills
my affection for little blue pills

Andy Capp, tenner wraps
All the blokes have bad backs
Druridge Bay, Giro day

If u read this u r gay
Gormans chips, tall ships
Mike Neville's liver, the Coquet river
Knotts flats, lost cats,
pensioners in baseball caps
pensioners in baseball caps

Ellington ponies, tea at Mark Toneys
Spuggy churches, primal urges
Rothley Crags, the Likely Lads
Here mate can a buy a tab
Super-strong weed, the Venerable Bede
From Old Bewick to Xmas at Fenwicks
The great Northumbrian coastal plain
To Bargain Booze in Percy Main
To Bargain Booze in Percy Main

Beadnell to Boulmer, bottles of Bella
Cambo and Duddo to Shields Road Wilkos
Lindisfarne, wind farms
Chucking out time at the Cumberland Arms
Alcan, the smoking ban,
Middle of winter ice cream vans
Kippers from Craster, I'm living on pasta
The New Hartley Pit Disaster
From Yeavering Bell to Meadowell

From Cuddy's Cave to me grandma's grave
From Kwiksave to me grandad's grave

Excerpts from **Small words from the great pause**

Spring-blue, silent sky
over silent interchange
blossom thick as snow

*

seagulls wheel in vain
fatty snacks in short supply
shuttered bakery

*

not seen much these days
pensioners at bus stops stood
blocking timetables

*

interrupted, pub
boarded up for weeks now, still
smells of cannabis

*

from the silhouettes
full moon arcs up, distancing
isolated, trapped

Catherine Graham

'I was born in Newcastle where I still live. Growing up in The Dwellings, I'd never heard of 'The Working Class' though I did wonder why there were never families like mine on BBC quiz shows like *Ask The Family*. My Da wasn't a doctor and my Mam wasn't a teacher, so we weren't expected to win any prizes other than at bingo or on the horses, right? What was I thinking of, to dream that I could win awards for my poetry?

I started to get myself along to local poetry nights. The first time I read on stage I was breathing so fast I was like an Olympic runner at the finishing line. The audience clapped loudly, some people stood up, I felt that I should apologise, as if I'd wangled my way into letting them think I was a real poet. The first time I got myself to a poetry masterclass, (I've never been to university) the tutor announced that we were to write a group sestina. I was asked, "Are you familiar with the form?" I did what any 'out of place' pupil would do and gave the daftest answer to get a laugh, "A urine infection?" Two people laughed, the others were too self-important to laugh.

I was determined after that night to write poems that speak to people, to have my moment—like Julia Roberts in that scene in *Pretty Woman* when she walks back into the posh shop where the staff had looked at her as if she'd been dropped in dog shite. The poetry world can be like that. I've seen 'elite' poets, the 'top brass' almost piped into the room like a haggis on Burns Night, the audience orgasmic, (fake of course) but obliged to deliver. That's not how it should be. Why this crazy hierarchy? Poetry is for everyone regardless of their class.'

Catherine Graham's poetry has been published in the UK, USA and Ireland as well as online. Her awards include The Jo Cox Poetry Award. Catherine's latest collection is Like A Fish Out Of Batter *(Indigo Dreams Publishing) and is inspired by the work of artist L. S. Lowry because, she says,* 'the people in his paintings could be my own family.'

Factory Outing

Yachts, 1959

Red and yellow sails like flames
out on the water; the salt-sea air

so good for factory girls like me,
girls who spend their days in overalls

and daft hats; busy little workers
pounding the production line.

The two blokes in row boats look
knackered, like *me* at the end of a shift.

My ex was at the back of the bus, sat
next to her from Packaging. God she was

packed into that dress. Maybe I'll just
stand here a bit longer, imagine life

beyond that horizon, but what the hell
do I know about life beyond any horizon,

standing here looking at yachts, feeling
lost, like a fish out of batter, praying

my period will come, either that or
with the next kind wave I drown.

Daughters of Tyne

I

Martha's neddin' bread rests
like a full moon on the scullery workbench,

the smell of warm dough
wafting along the passage to the end room

where Nancy keeps her savings
in a yellow-white chest of drawers.

She has no idea that every Monday,
my mother borrows a pound note,

promising herself she'll replace it by Friday,
before Nancy clocks off at the liver salts factory.

Many a time it's a photo finish between Nancy
getting off the bus and mam replacing the note.

By October, mother permitting,
there'll be enough for the wedding.

II

Edie has never married, never met
the man of her dreams, a man who

plays for United and bleeds black
and white. He has a quiff like Elvis

and a voice like Pat Boon: smokes filter tip
cigarettes. He is as hard as December

and gentle as July; slightly bow-legged
with a glint in his eye like Russ Conway.

If ever he swears he puts tuppence in the cuss box.
Romance is played down for love is

carrying the coal up three flights of stairs.
There will be two children, a boy

who can kick a ball like his father
and a girl who can kick even higher.

III

The women I grew up with had
tell it like it is voices. They favoured vowels,

vowels that flex mouths
like opera singers limbering up for an aria.

They made soup from bones and knitted
anything from booties to balaclavas.

Bless them, for they breastfed their babies
and had bairns vaccinated via sugar cubes.

The women I knew made their feelings known
in a clash of pans. Always there

at the school gates, their headscarves
blowing like flags in the biting northeasterly wind.

They believed in the Bible and best butter
and knew by heart, their Co-op dividend number.

My Father Never Got Over
Being Voted Off the Allotments

He pictured them sitting around the table
like a green-fingered séance: the committee.
Well-pruned men and women, women who
step out of the bath to break wind and men
who wash and polish their cars every Sunday.
"That's how they live in them leafy suburbs,"
he used to say, "that's their Sunday dinner."
He hadn't time for committees; hadn't time
for smarmy men or gaffers who play the game
of "If it was up to *me* lads." He hadn't time for
the way pitmen were portrayed in the media,
"Miners wouldn't swear like that in front of bairns."

I remember how we would sit, Sunday nights
around the small table by the fire, how Da could
take seven dominoes and hold them in one hand,
how he'd smile at my mother and say so much,
so much without saying a word. They broke him
when the factory found him "light duties" until
at fifty they gave him his cards. That weekend
was a scorcher, I see him still, in his pale green
shirt, sleeves rolled up to his elbows, his frayed
seventeen inch open collar. He came home from
the allotment with the letter, the smell of panhaggerty
in the oven, the taste of a final Sunday on his tongue.

Putting Aunt Adeline On the Train

Head of a Woman in a Feathered Hat

I'd never tried cheese and pineapple
until I met Aunt Adeline;

never seen a real feather in a hat.
I thought perfume smelled of violets

and petticoats were flannelette.
Until I met Aunt Adeline

I'd never heard of South Africa,
anyone coming to visit came from Blyth.

But I learned so much in that fortnight,
so much about a different life.

As her train steamed away from the station
I asked my mother, 'Mam, what's *apartheid*?'

And Mam, like a ventriloquist and still waving,
'Fasten your coat, you look cold,' replied.

A Protest March
after the painting by L.S. Lowry

Get out of the road, dogs!

They're coming, marching

but this lot aren't from

the factories, they're too

well dressed, too high

and mighty to carry banners.

They're obviously in ranks,

big knobs first. One or two

women add a token red

to the black and grey prism.

But why my street? Why

not take the scenic route

instead? Scenic my arse.

They just want us to see

power on the move. This

is no protest, more a march.

Not a sound from neighbours

as they stand still and watch.

The men bow their heads,

one man stands erect!

Silly buggers, it's politics

not a bloody funeral march.

Shift

Going to Work, 1959

The only shadows you see around here
are the five o'clock ones on faces.

Shift workers up at the crack of
fried bacon on days, up in time for last orders

on nights. I don't need an alarm clock,
not with next door's squawking kids.

I never want kids; never want to be
a father, I'd rather bat for the other team

than turn out like my old man. He can
go to hell. All I wanted was a bit of fun,

she knew the score, where's the harm?
I might have told her she was special

and Christ, she was. But I never made
any promises: I never mentioned love.

Head of A Young Man in a Cap
after the painting by L.S. Lowry

He looks posh even in his flat cap.
His mouth reminds me of a pen pal I had

when I was a girl. He was twenty-one,
I was too young so I sent him photos

of our Shirley instead. He sent me poems
in blue envelopes stamped, *Par Avion.*

I'd read them in bed and imagine him
looking into my eyes and whispering

Par Avion. I took on a different persona;
pretended to smoke and shrugged my shoulders.

He was happy for me to write in English
and sometimes he would do the same.

Letters from France fizzled out like a sparkler.
There were fireworks when my father found out.

He asked me, 'Who the hell's Serge?'
I pretended I hadn't heard. He asked me again

and threw the letters in the fire. I told him
he was no-one as under my breath I muttered, *Merde.*

I Beg to Apply for the Post
after Jack Common, 1903—1968

My school was tough:
the teachers weighed in,
tipping the scales with their red pencils,
their toxic, chalk dust.
I beg to apply for the post.

Like you, my father learned shorthand;
attended evening class at the colliery.
A cacophony of skills, don't you think?
Like my mother, singing opera in the scullery.
Beware of the man who wants marriage,
isn't that what you told your readers?
My father taught me to ride a bike
and not depend on stabilizers.
He hated smarmy men the most.
I beg to apply for the post.

No silver spoons in our house.
Our doorstep was donkey-stoned.
We refused to be shoved into snobbery,
refused to give up the ghost
when they refurbished The Dwellings
and named it Millennium Court.
Ashes to ashes, communities to dust.
I beg to apply for the post.

I've never failed to fit in,
never lived in a 'culture vacuum'.
Why, our backlane was a canvas
to the local graffiti artist.
I beg to apply for the post.

Brought up on Dickman's pies
but I never mince my words.
I don't give anything I don't want to.
I don't go about hard-faced.
I'm not fighting any class war
in silk-lined, kid gloves:
I have a voice, I haven't lost faith.
I'm taking on life bare knuckled,
this kiddar's luck has changed.

I don't believe in the twaddle
I read in most of the papers.
I know when to tell the truth;
when to spout the necessary lie.
I learned all this at my cost—
I beg to apply for the post.
I would supply references
from my previous employer
though, fair to say there was no love lost.
He had ideas above my station;
his wife was all fur coat.
More edge than a broken piss pot.
I beg to apply for the post.

I pride myself on being punctual;
always on the dot.
I don't pretend or hope to be
what I'm definitely not.
I tick all of the boxes,
I call salmon paté, salmon paste.
I know my place but I don't like to boast.
I beg to apply for the post.

Joan Johnston

'When I was 13 my Nanna died. Secretly I tried to write about her. I thought I ought to call her my Grandmother. I didn't know it was OK to write about the way she used to spit into the back of the fire and make it sizzle. Or how I'd miss her smell. From my reading —I did a lot of reading—I already knew that writing poetry was something other people did. People I didn't know. People who didn't live in the north-east of England. People whose dads definitely didn't read *The Football Pink*.

For a long time I allowed the expectations of others to influence my own. Who was I to think I could write? And what was I going to write about? I never seemed to have the right kind of Writerly Experiences. Holidays in caravans, school dinners, the contents of mam's kitchen cupboards... these were not the stuff of Literature. So I carried on reading other people's stories instead. And secretly writing.

It wasn't until I plucked up the courage to join a creative writing group in Newcastle in the mid 1980s (affordable! free crèche!) that I met other writers whose backgrounds and experiences matched my own. We recognised and supported each other, began to tell our own stories, in our own words, and our confidence grew.

Looking around on the internet it seems the mainstream publishing gatekeepers are beginning to notice that working-class writers are missing from their lists. It's about time—for the sake of readers as well as writers. More than ever now, we need a diversity of voices to be given the opportunity to tell their stories. The working class is made up of a range of communities after all.

I'm pleased to have been invited to offer some of my poems for this anthology. My Nanna would be pleased for me too. A bit baffled perhaps, and probably worried about what the neighbours might think, but pleased.'

Joan Johnston was born in Newcastle and lives on Tyneside. She has worked as a writer in schools, hospitals and prisons, and with women's groups, the elderly and the homeless. She teaches creative writing on a freelance basis and in Adult Education. Since 1998 she has published three poetry pamphlets and three collections (with Flarestack, Midnag, Diamond Twig press, dogeater press, Red Squirrel Press) and is widely published in anthologies and magazines.

The Girl Caught

They day they caught me
being Cilla Black
I was back-combed
and miming into my hairbrush,
standing on a chair,
performing into a mirror
above the sideboard.
Mam said she worried
about my balance, the way I reached
for the high notes at the end.

The day they caught me
creeping out the door
with my Beatle skirt,
Beatle jumper,
Beatle boots
and a bottle of hair-straightener
stuffed inside my Beatle bag
I was headed for Brenda's
to do our Beatle fringes,
get changed
and go to the Maj,
to meet those two lads
who both looked like George.

The day they caught me
cheating in class,
sneaking a peep
at capital cities
on a list up my sleeve,
I blamed Janet
who was sitting beside me,
quietly copying all my answers.

And if Janet suggested
jumping off the Tyne Bridge
would you do it?
Miss McGowan asked.
No Miss I lied,
immediately picturing us
holding hands,
balancing on a girder
in floating white dresses,
swallow-diving together
into the river.

Reproduction

On the other side of the humpbacked
bridge, through the dank of its arch,

past the rag-and-bone-man's yelping
pups in his caravan in the scrapyard,

to Mucky Pool where she told me
the facts, used a stick to draw

the details in dirt, damp soil,
where she held me down, had me

lapping the warm-skinned
water on and on until

somehow it's been years
and I find this place persisting

in views across those vanished fields
that conjure themselves daily,

in a close-up printed behind my eyes
of the house she once lived in,

in this zoom shot that makes me look up
from the book I thought I was reading:

her arms open wide in a bloom
of blue algae, floating.

Remix

remembering Jean, 1967

You make an entrance tonight
with a different spin
—you've discovered the sarong,

body glitter, Marlboro Lights,
fast-drying nail polish.
You're saying things

you never said: *This Dyson's
changed my life. His tea's
defrosting in the mike*

then we're off on the Metro,
together at last,
to Billy Botto's in Byker

where I'm old enough now
to be allowed in
and you're still not a day over forty;

where they're playing this new release
and I see what I used to imagine
—your bleached hair falling loose

as you mouth the words, expertly
smooch with James Bond in a blazer,
to Satchmo.

Ada in Autumn

in her old sandals, her favourite gold earrings with the turquoise stone,
is coming down the back lane from her overgrown allotment,

heading for home in a rising gale with two plastic carrier bags
bulging with windfalls. We meet by her gate where she leans her stick,

steadies herself, then fills my coat pockets, my rucksack, my arms
with bronze pears and green apples, saying, *'Here pet, have some of these*

Under 11s

Little Sharkey has to come off:
studded again down the back of his leg,
man-to-man marked by their number 5
who keeps going in hard

but the only sub left is Spud, shivering
in a pair of second-hand Predators,
so Sharkey limps back on.
I want to kiss him. His dad never comes.

As I rinse his blood out of the sponge
Big Rob shouts *Howay lads!*
Youse are playing like tarts.

Maybe this'll be the day

when the boat sails up Bottle Bank,
when I'll glance up from the scullery sink
to see the Swing Bridge opening, the pigeons
all turning into pigs that fly. Maybe
today's the day when that big boat
will float over the cobbles
and dock at the end of Saltwell Road,
spill into my lap its cargo of
shoes for the bairns, work for the men,
a new leg for Bob, best butter from the country,
one bonny little bottle of Evening in Paris,
fresh elbow grease.

Fathers of the early 50's

We saw them on Sundays from our prams,
their faces framed by empty skies:

the breeze at their backs
they pushed us out,

one hand gripping the handle,
a Navy Cut in the other, directed

under the curved palm, held between thumb
and middle fingertip. Protected

from changes in the weather we watched them
as they squinted ahead, and we looked out

at what had just passed—purple fireweed
growing through broken brickwork,

all the new-laid lawns with tidy edges
they'd mow and trim when we got back,

the climbing roses they'd hold us up to.

Ben Sherman or What are you doing wanting a lad's shirt anyway?

Deep-pink cotton. Button-down collar. Loop at the back. Pleat.
In an attempt to straighten my Pansticked face
she's bought me a fake from C&A's
and I'll never get away with it, how will I get away
tonight, sneak out in my threadbare-but-at-least-it's-credible
Brutus Trim-Fit instead? She'll be checking
at the door. *So come on, let's see it then*
and she is. *Honestly, it looks lovely pet*
and no-one will ever know the difference.
69/11d just for a shirt! Ben Who?
Oh, that youth cub dance I never went into. Bottled it
—had no choice. Said goodbye to any chance with Trev or Dave
or Mod Tom (gorgeous, I heard, in a brand new yellow one),
had to keep my three-quarter lengthy maroon leather coat on
and hang about clock-watching all night in the church porch
with Existential Pete from the Upper 6th
—horn-rimmed specs and a bulky jumper, a practising
Outsider, though to his credit he really was
inhaling all those Players Number 6—
who quoted me Camus in the original French, at some length,
before resorting to a pompous, posh Geordie:
History is made, Joan, and never bought
then lapsing, finally, into the desperate authentic
—something about the importance of *ploughing*
wor own furrows, so how about it?

A Song of Addison

Two long streets of back-to-back birches. High Row, Low Row—
overgrown addresses
lost to nettles, accumulations of moss and lichen, the fallen

leaves no wind reaches. At the mouth of the old pit tunnel your dog
hears the voices:
ghost-notes behind its bricked up throat.

** The mining village of Addison in Gateshead was abandoned in the 1950s.
It was well known for its male voice choir.*

On Falling Up Dog Leap Stairs

Already your tongue's checked
your front teeth twice. One shin
is stinging, your forehead's intact

but those minutes you'd saved, precious
coins in your pocket, lie spent
on the steps. You notice your legs

have you upright gain, and your feet,
ignoring the interruption,
have carried you on—suede-booted,

weightless—but now they've given in.
You're on your own, half-way up,
illuminated by a yellow lamp.

You hold on to what's left of your breath
then slowly exhale, listening for footsteps
not coming, still

not coming out of the dark, the silence above
and behind your thudding pulse. In the beats between
you offer a deal to the ancient

hiding close by, watching. Then you stop
having thoughts—you make a move, go
with what the shadow-cat in you knows, in her bones.

Kathleen Kenny

Serfdom & Poetry

'In 1861 Russia's serfs were officially emancipated, almost thirty-five percent of the country's population considered no more than possessions: chattels who could be bought and sold. As someone living in the twenty-first century it's easy to believe this happened so far back in time that it's become ancient history. But to put it in prospective, this Great Emancipation, as it's known, occurred only three decades before my dad's birth. The plight of these people brought a sense of connection and empathy which endured with him all his life.

My dad made many links between the working classes of the British Isles into which he was born and Russian serfdom. When it came right down to it, he saw all the lowly born as being, essentially, owned. An opinion formed from his own experiences of hard, soul-destroying labour, and of being sent as a youth into the hellholes of WW1's Western Front. His distrust of Authority and profound cynicism were lifelong, and live on in me.

I count myself fortunate. As it turns out the mid-twentieth century, into which I arrived, afforded the working classes much greater opportunities, some of which I was able to take advantage of. But that which can be given can also be taken away—so let's take nothing for granted.

When I first came to writing in the late 80s, my hometown of Newcastle enjoyed a thriving, free thinking, creative scene open to all-comers. Sadly, the ubiquitous rise of university-based degree courses oversaw its demise. The smell of money-making was in the air and soon this type of creative freedom was absorbed into various 'hallowed-halls'. A lot of the writing produced today reflects poorly on this. Because no matter what ingredients you put into a sausage machine the same result ensues: strings of sausages.

These days I count myself an outsider, way beyond futile attempts to impress innumerable string-pullers, purse-holders or favour-bestowers—exercises in masochism if ever there were. These days I write freely without fear or favour, and inevitably with zero chance of making money. Without doubt though, this is the best and most creative time of my life. I thank my forebearers for all their teaching. I thank them daily, and humbly, for my unearned privileges, and for all I continue to learn about their times and lives.'

Medicine

Before you can think, metal moves past
your lips, presses a still stone of tongue.

You don't know what you've done,
try to control the urge to choke,

an impulse to throw up on the shiny
implement shaped like a crescent moon.

Tickling your throat, the mixture
treacles through your belly,

soothing, cooling, healing:
the answer to everything.

Momentarily.

Cleaning

Taking down the nets,
fingerprints lifted
clean off the patio set.

Scrubbed from the lino,
from the rim of each sink;
scorched within an inch

of existence:
everything that was,
everything that passed.

A Place of Loss

She forgot things can be kept for weeks.
These days a loaf takes forever to mould.

Back then she ate homemade bread,
hard as rock, no preservatives.

Her mother in the kitchen cutting off
green crusts, blue and white spots from cheese.

She remembered she forgot;
drank tea from the tall white cup,

burned her lip that still hurt
because of what happened.

She woke to find herself again,
dusting, bathing, filing fingernails,

watching TV; reading about another war,
yet more insane insanity.

Solitary

For the first time, cooking,
shopping, washing for one;

marveling at your pained
reflection, strangely enlarged.

This new place of old mirrors,
their glaze of tarnished greens.

Not cleaning anything at all,
or ironing a centre crease

into someone else's jeans.

Pre

Before the bitterness,
before the resentment,
before such and such a man
was the biggest bastard
ever to walk on two legs,

let's leave him
with a large Hungarian tashe,
holding his new born son
or having just done the shopping
or mowing the lawn
or kissing his woman's toes
or sowing a tear in her dress.

Let's leave him playing the hero,
talking down a suicidal boy,
or scaling a tree to save a cat,
grappling with its long red coat
plastered to his well-oiled chest.

What the Tannoy Says

The world is full of plastic fruit
and it's rotting. Rats nibble

at papier-mâché women
who can't think but lash out

with handbags full of bricks,
roses of blood on their robes.

Was that hay or fish,
one black leg, one broken hip?

What should we make of it,
this relentless progressive plod?

How to convert a sitting room
into a sitting room,

a kitchen into a kitchen,
an upper flat into a luxurious penthouse.

Blueprint for a Big House
Annaghmakerrig

Hard to say, how long it's been this way,
everything laid on a plate.
Sun up over the cooking range,
pots of every size and shape,
stainless steel utensils,
their steamy dish-washed haze.

On the blink, the blue fly zapper,
which has been a reliable executioner,
dribbles a web of indelible ink
into the grain of the polished floor,
into the glint of sunshine on the sink.

From nowhere, off-kilter,
the smell of the old piggery. Maps,
illuminating time past, tilting
the drawing room walls. Life studies.
Portraits of important men pointing the way
they and their comely wives will lead.

Spirits transcending death,
set in the weave of the house,
in the fabric of the cushioned alcoves.
So that all who follow here will wonder,
and never truly know, how it was
to be alive, before our stellar strides:

the progress we made,
the lifestyles we own.

Faith

If she tells you this is blue
you must believe it.
Abandoned dolls don't lie,
see her dinted face,
her sucked out eyes,
her bones worn like old shoes.

See this knitted Christ,
this chalk Virgin,
this cup of tea made
from a deconstructed kettle;
this meal of salted down bull
reconstituted by Saint Donard

in his Mourne Mountain hideout:
mountains of my mother's birth,
place of saints and sinners,
a place she wouldn't care to grace
with the romantic name of home.

Badger Cull

Inside rooms of blue shadow
waves of green breath stretch
from kitchen cupboards to grey walls
then out to where the woods are wild;

where scurrying tails tempt starved cats
with eyes that have been scrubbed
until they squeak, gold and black,
stealthy, clearcut, clean.

Brown wire, electrified threads,
life generating heat:
one type of whiskered creature
contemplates the death of another.

Thinking of Everything

A bird beats itself against the glass.
A twitching cat looks up,
stretches her paws across the low stone wall.

A fat bulldog drags its owner home
like a doomed ox off to the slaughter house.
It wants to kill the cat. It wants to eat the pigeon.

It wants to piss against the brick building
I am wrapped inside, toes squeezing
a pink satin quilt, hands seeking again

Dad's shoddy wartime blanket.
And for the first time in life,
my eyes acquiring 20/20 vision.

The army frequently used a type of material called shoddy to make its blankets. This material is ground up to form a fibrous material that is re-spun into very rough yarn and made into blankets.

The Gravel Road to Memory

Bus fumes and blossom
mingle over churchyard bones
lying beneath concentric circles
of small white stones
that show us
the way back to the centre.

Old burial grounds:
the everyday of lost children.
Human defeat borne deep.
Irresistible draw to earth.
This equality of dirt.

What became of us,
our eyes dried and cracked
from mourning youth,
sweeping cobbles, heaping dust,
filth on the hems of our skirts?

Playground of the Sacred Heart

The wind, the wind, the wind blows higher,
in comes Kathleen from the Sky-er;
isn't she beautiful, isn't she sweet,
tell me the boy that she might meet:

Terence Finnegan says he loves her,
John O'Shea says he loves her,
Steven Ashton says he loves her.
Is it true or is it false?

True, false.   True, false.   True!

The wind, the wind, the wind blows higher,
in comes Kathleen from the Sky-er;
isn't she beautiful, isn't she sweet,
tell me the boy that she might meet:

Joseph Bulman says he loves her,
Michael Pearce says he loves her,
Tubby Spinks says he loves her.
Is it true or is it false?

True, false.   True, false.   False!

Lisa Matthews

'Growing up, poetry was something I wrote in secret. There were no poets or artists where I lived, although tradesmen worked in wood and steel and stone, making and mending. My father's skill as a joiner has left a deep impression on me. With a few bits of wood he can make miraculous, wonderful things. He can find the shape of the grain and for me carpentry and poetry have always felt intimately entwined.

In 1986 I read '45 Mercy Street' by the US poet Anne Sexton. That moment changed my life. Forever. At that point I'd not read much poetry, if any, by women. I was nineteen years of age and Sexton's voice made me realise, for the very first time, that I could be a poet. About three years after the Sexton discovery I lost a very close friend to cancer. She died quickly, and all of a sudden I was exposed to my own mortality at, I think, way too young an age. After her funeral I remember sitting thinking: if this had been me, what would I regret not doing? I knew the answer before I asked the question. And this is why I became a poet.

I am a poet because words, their sounds in the mouth and on the air, their form and aesthetic on the page still seem like the most ordinary kind of magic. Poetry has never felt complicated to me. When words fail me, I turn to poetry; either the reading or the writing of it. Because it seems to me that poetry, perhaps more than any art form, can express the inexpressible. Poetry speaks from the heart to the heart, and it is vital for a life well-lived.'

Gabriel Nesbit always has something to say

The new school year starts late, and I haven't
seen Gabriel all summer.

During the first assembly our Headmaster
says we should pray for all the hungry
children around the world who do not have
families or proper houses to live in.

After tea, I run down to Cruddas Park and pick
up the intercom in the tiled entrance of
Gabriel's flats.

*Come in Gabriel Nesbitt, Gabriel Nesbitt do
you read me?*

The intercom is silent, except for an empty
hiss that continues for as long as I hold the
receiver to my ear.

I call on Gabriel a few times.

Then, after a few days of not going, I decide
to try one more time.

There is the usual sssssssssssss of ssstatic, then
a click and someone breathing.

The double door next to the intercom buzzes
and the big lock makes a thick metallic sound.

But I do not push it and I do not go in.

I just hold the receiver away from my ear and
wait for Gabriel to say something, because
Gabriel Nesbitt always had something to say.

Tower blocks

Somewhere the final smudge of paraffin
inches down the can.

The bell over the shop door jangles. The
counter. The pen knives. The flypapers and

carpet tacks. Stripper to get rid of Shellac. On
Sundays we all walk to mass. The streets

coming down like a bad cough around us.
There are rats. Council traps. My mother

drowns one that's been injured in a Marvel
tin. The smell of brick dust, sharp sand and

mortar. The day Jack and me broke a new
window to get a fiver that was lying on a

newly-skimmed floor. Fenced-off diggers.
Kids we don't know let all the handbrakes

off and as they rumble towards Armstrong
Road, Jack and me start to run. Not out of

guilt or fear, but because we could—because
we could run. All the way to Cruddas Park

where the flats stand tall against the sky.
Everyone is out on the street,

'London Calling' playing on the radios.

Grasshopper Hill

Where the grass sweeps up from Buddle Road
and the cemetery has two voices.

Where you can see the street party and the
streamers threading up the lanes.

Where you walked to school through the sun,
through the leaves, through conver-

-sations about a woman Prime Minister.

Where you held and then let go of your
mother's hand.

Where the man from the pie shop walked his
dog. The dog had four legs. Then three.

Where the light was brilliant.

Where the fields were ours, as I curled up one
corner of a boiled egg sammidge.

Where I cried alone when my Grandfather
died.

Where the gates always closed at dusk.

Where dust was the signal of day's end and of
bedtime with new blankets in a shared

single room.

Where everything was present, present and
held perfectly in time.

Backyard

Over the wall Mrs Edwards swears at kids who
moved away years ago. The dishes on the
drainer stand in the afternoon sun. The
backyard a promise stretching out down the
lane and on to the river. Everyone's gone to
the terrace to watch the bands. When you
think of it, life is a piece of paper you stuff in
your pocket—these words written on it:
granny, caravan, gone-to-the-housey. You
remember the first can of Coca Cola brazen
as a pillar box in Joan's corner shop. It sets
your teeth on edge when you had a swig from
the girl at the bus stop. That winter I walked
the top road into Elswick then on to the Blue
Lamp to look for Dad who wasn't back from
work. The snow had been ploughed to the
sides and was as high as the fences on the
houses with gardens. Down the hill the sky as
red as the can on the shelf.

Kitchen sinks
(after 'Carl and the Empties', a photograph by Tish Murtha)

I. Ullswater

My grandmother says no to me all the time, and it's such a small word I suppose it doesn't mean much to her. The garden lies beyond us, and ripping feathers from the chicken she has already decided I am no good. The bird's head hangs over the edge, its eyes set to the off position. I have grown. Outside, my cousin swings up into the sunlight shiving over the privet, the silver buckles on her yellow sandals coursing on-to-off, off-to-on, like a buoy in deep water.

II. Caroline

My mother colours her hair at the kitchen sink. She looks at herself in my father's shaving mirror. There is brown paste on the skin at the back of her neck. She takes me in her arms and holds me for a long time, smoothing her hand over the top of my head. Then she lets go and I return to the back yard and throw a tennis ball against the wall. Through the window I can see her dark eyes settling on the space between her face and its circular reflection.

III. Carl

He holds the bag open, and puts a bottle in. Each one on the drainer a message filled with morning, its blue star settled and ready to leave on their long flight. The street, a procession of paving stones, holds its breath as everywhere voices lift like birds, like light. Sometimes when I stop to listen, the day is just amazing. Each door a life, each story one of a kind, each family a supernova of possibility exploding across the west end sky.

Ally May

'I live and write in Newcastle.

There is a part of the book Britannia Unchained written in 2012 by four current Tory cabinet ministers that says *'once they enter the workplace, British workers are among the worst idlers in the world'*.

In the same book it says that 'instead of wanting to be a doctor or a businessman the British are more interested in football and pop music.'

Growing up I never really had any artistic ambitions, in fact I was sacked from the school play for fidgeting in rehearsals. It was only when I was on the cusp of adulthood that I started being interested in books, as opposed to football and pop music.

Sometimes being told you can't do something makes you all the more determined to do it.'

August night

The six of us run to play havoc
with the swings
in Paddy Freemans.
I am wearing my shirt outside my jeans.
Neil tries to wreck a stranger's garden party
by shouting "we're geordies
we're mental
we're fucking off we're heads".

August

We play pool in the monkey bar at 4pm on a Sunday afternoon
while drinking Stella and watching football on tv.

We know that in a few months' time we will be doing the same
except in the dark.

St. James' Park

During the stadium tour
we saw the bushes
that said NUFC
and Tommy Cassidy's' shirt
from the league cup final
behind glass.

The Duke

I am sitting in the window
of The Duke
watching people hurry by
in the sleet
with late nineties indie
coming out of the speakers
with half a pint left in
pint glass
trying to make peace
with the past
while Chelsea beat
Tottenham silently
in the background.

Westgate Road

We drink in the third storey
of a sandstone building near the station,

watch taxis and stag and hen parties pass by.
When it is time to leave it starts to rain and gets dark.

Strike pay

Malcolm said his garden
never looked
better than in '84.
He had no money
to go anywhere
or do anything.
Every time a weed
came through
he got rid of it.

Five nil

Who scores the fifth?
It's Phillipe Albert!
(He speaks with a Geordie accent).
When he chips Schmeichel
beer flies in the air.

There is an

empty chair in the Lit and Phil.
a place going spare
in the Blaydon race
and blossom on the ground
knocked off trees by rain.

In early autumn

the sunlight on red berries
casting shadows
and on leaves flickering
through the blinds
on the carpet.

Hoppings '86

Hodgey says we are going to
get our heads stoved in
by kids from Whitley.
I spot two girls from my year
and wish my dark blue shirt
hadn't been in the wash.
Someone ruins 'Sinful', by Pete Wylie
by talking through a microphone.
At dusk our
cider flashes like a siren
in its gold bottle.

Paul Summers

'I was born into an old mining terrace which was inhabited completely by a legion of grey-haired and black-lunged storytellers, balladeers, fantasists and singers. As soon as they thought I was capable of comprehension they bombarded me with their spoken histories, their songs, their gossip and their ghosts, their lies and their truths. I lapped it up, insatiable.

It was almost inevitable I'd become a teller of tales myself, a teller of tales about us and our peers, about the communities we lived and that were quickly disappearing. I imagined myself as some strange hybrid existing somewhere between John Boy Walton and Alan Hull, and so I wrote things down: ordinary, beautiful, sad, rage-filled, moving things that happened around me and to me.'

bun stop

hail the starlings
of amen corner,
their anarchy
tamed by the pulse
of murmuration.

hail the melody
of stone & brick,
of bulging glass,
these jaded domes
& gilded spires.

hail the rhythms
of footfall & heart,
the blood & sweat
of struggles spent
& yet to pass.

hail the tension
in this puddle's skin,
the fragile dialectic
of gravity & mass,
its face bow-taut,
each stance conflicted.

hail to the hoar
on the cobble's pout,
these gutters choked
with poet's whimsy,
hubris & votives,
rhetoric floundering
in the lort burn's swill.

hail sycophant & sage,
the muddle of denial,
cold land of lad
& bloated laird,
of thrones usurped
or quietly vacant.

hail these bridges
& the arc of their stature.
hail the municipal
& the muted keep.

hail snowdrop & bluebell
& the toll of our losses.
republic of goose-bump
& high street dandy,
fiefdom of magpie
& impotent ghosts;
each spurt of growth
constricted by romance.

hail this dance
of scant advancement,
the cadence of decay
in the tyne's chill madrigal.
confluence of meme & gene;
each artery clogged.

hail the kittiwakes
of spillers' mill,
proclaiming their prayer
to fractured dawn,
a clutch of notes
to do their bidding.

faking springtime

for half a year, this city has sworn itself to greyness,
ganged up with the weather to terrorise rheumatics.

at 6.37 this morning though, when he coughed himself awake
there was cloudless blue through the crack in the curtains,

through the crack in his eyelids, & a sparrow,
whistling the theme tune from mission impossible:

yesterday's clothes are heaped like sand dunes,
the legacy of her perfume suggesting flowers.

6.43 a.m., greyness resumed, sparrow silenced,
the helpless sun eclipsed by cloud, the clatter of hail.

while they were sleeping, the damp patch on the ceiling
has grown into a map of the dardanelles.

the last bus:

i. the last bus

one more tedious chorus
of *suck my cocks*
& i'll be back—
back to the bookends,
the balding pebble-dash
of once-home,
to mam asleep,
& dad squinting at the match

ii. pompeii

the door will be open.
familiar stairs will greet me;
still a slither of carpeted pyramid,
still the summit of everest,
still a mystery despite all
my subsequent reasoning.
beyond, my pompeii:
a museum of bunk-beds
& scrap-books neatly housed
on formica shelves,
a squadron of airfix planes
so heavy with dust
that they are grounded.

iii. silent movie

there will be
no spoken welcomes;
perhaps a patted shoulder,
a general enquiry of mutual well-being,
an offer of alcohol or tea,
but mainly the silence
of expressionless love.
tomorrow he will bury his father.

iv. breakfast

undeterred by the seriousness
of it all, i tease mam about the
instant coffee; i have spent my
lifetime teasing their sensibilities,
made it my duty to talk politics
at every shared meal, bored them
to tears with history's injustice
& the rhetoric of struggle: not once
have i sat here just to eat. always
canvassing for approval, always
the missionary, so rarely the son.

v. eulogy

for three months they had sat like sentries
at the foot of his bed, watched him shrink,
made sense of jumbled words, poured
hundreds of glasses of lucozade,
smiled at him effortlessly when his eyes
opened briefly & at each other when they
closed again. they never missed a day.

vi. taboo

her words were like a sad old song,
each pathetic line choking her.
she spoke about dad, & how
at granda's passing he had uttered
those words: three times he'd said
i love you, his hands climbing his
father's chest like a child wanting
to be carried. it had been an hour
or more before he could see to drive.

vii. history

he had known nothing but outside toilets,
grown accustomed to draughts; thinking
our place posh with its upstairs lav. a relic
of before. he had known the harshness
of strikes, & of begging to the guardians
for a vestige of their charity, he had seen
men crushed like ripe fruit by falls of rock,
been blinded by shift-end light for almost
fifty years, & all this time a dream recurred,
a patchwork of cowboys borrowed from
libraries, of heroes with his face. he had
done without beer for weeks to buy dad's
first bike & was rarely impressed by hardship.
he was generous with his smiles, but never
to my knowledge ever once kissed my grandma:
his spine was bent, his lungs full, each scar he had,
a blue tattoo, & since his retirement he bathed
once a week & shopped nowhere but the co-op
despite mam's constant nagging.

viii. witness

witness the scarce embrace
of brothers; in doing well,
grown separate. witness
the puzzled heirs to a half built
jerusalem, guilty only of potential.
witness the prophecy of a single
hybrid rose, dedicated to memory,
without perfume or thorns.
witness the past, respectfully
collected at twelve careful paces;
in their parochial eyes, our ring
of blood an ivy league huddle.

ix. prodigals

we are prodigals
too long away
the orphans of nostalgia
all our singular pasts
un-spendable currency
we are stranded
& this hearse
the last bus

st. gloria's day

it's finally official: the pope has
confirmed it in a multi-lingual
coda to the good friday mass.
the canonisation of gloria
gaynor as the patron-saint of
battered wives; her motto the
latin for 'i will survive'. it
reminds me of this woman i
talked to in kwiksave as i
queued for tobacco at pre-
budget prices. she wore a neat
group of crescent scars where
he'd planted the gold of his half-
sovereign ring squarely on the
curve of her blushered left
cheek, astoundingly consistent
for someone so pissed: more
accurate than william tell. she
hummed that song as we
waited in line, each monotone
burst a boast, a prayer.

art lesson

this terrace has taught thousands
their sense of perspective:
in fewer words & with less conceit.
a joy to draw: a simple clutch of lines,
two ups, two downs & with no fancy porticos.
more relevant, more graspable,
more obvious than a shelf of books,
a theatre queue, a field of sheep;
a boulevard of broken dreams.
let them sketch this: this street of ghosts,
& smudge the windows of imperfect pasts.
let them use rulers, & only three colours:
a dirty red, a gloss slate grey,
the carbon black of detail.
let them learn from a wall of clay.
let them watch as it disappears.

north.
(home thoughts from abroad)

we are more than sharply contrasting photographs
of massive ships and staithes for coal, more than
crackling films where grimy faced workers are
dwarfed by shadows or omitted by chimneys, more
than foul mouthed men in smoky clubs or well-built
women in a wash-day chorus. we are more than
lessons in post-industrial sociology, more than
just case-studies of dysfunctional community.
we are more than non-speaking extras in
fashionable new gangster movies, more than
sad lyrics in exiles songs. we are more than
the backbone of inglorious empire, or the
stubborn old heart of a dying beast. we are
more than the ghosts of a million histories,
more than legends inscribed in blood, more
than exhibits in some vast museum, or the
unbought remnants of a year-long sale,
we are more than this, but not much more.

face ache

as his brother mick so rightly said,
davey these days is a *miserable twat,*

developed a resistance to all forms of mirth,
can't even manage the slightest of grins

at the sight of a baby biting someone's nose,
doesn't flinch a muscle at the best told jokes:

tommy, who's his neighbour, & currently
enrolled on a night-class in counselling,

summed it up nicely in the lounge bar of the percy
between two rapid gobfuls of well-pulled guinness,

cheer your fucking face up man,
there's plenty more fish in the sea!

january song

there, like a cryptic clue to all our dumb histories,
the dog-shit footprints head off into the distance:

& yesterday's hockle has dried like sulphur
on the plateau of a traffic calming ramp.

the wind carries heartbreak, a swirl of chinese whispers,
a symphony of lover's names in the sighing of air-brakes.

of all glimpsed detail in wintertime's ambiguous light
only these are certainties: our skin will grow loose,
our bones melt.

the butcher's craft

the butcher's wife is beautiful.
irish, i think, from that singing lilt:
hardly surprising he bagged such a catch,
a man with a trade, an ancient craft—
his deft knife skating on the rind,
his stitching immaculate.

later, in their humid bathroom,
he double-checks a lump on her breast,
his strong hands reading the curves,
a tender smile masking fear,
the smell of meat still on his fingers.

bird

lunch-time mourners gather,
congealing like storm-cloud
on the wet pavement.
a pigeon, beak bleeding

& broken-winged,
circles like a toreador
in the city's muck.
the man with white hair

steps out from the crowd
& checking around him
for children's eyes,
gently snaps its neck.

judgement day

it's baking hot. we regret wearing coats.
from the slit top-deck window of a 39 bus
a skinny, ginger kid in a *kappa* tracksuit
shouts *paki cunts* at two old arabs.
the gobful of *pepsi* he spits at them
blows back, narrowly misses our bags.
he mutters sorry when i stare. there is
a crusty glue-sore on his bottom lip, &
his skin is overly pink, like a wax crayon.
his two fat mates obviously think he's cool:
they laugh their tits off at his every move,
taking tokes off the *regal kingsize* they'd
bummed just then from the pipe-cleaner
woman with bleached blonde hair. they
smoke it like a spliff, sucking 'til their
cheeks collapse, & blowing mis-shaped
smoke-rings over our heads. they look
like urang-utangs, especially the ginger one.

english breakfast

wrestling the perfume of frying eggs,
a trace of whisky orbits *The Sun.*

it is bastille day & the pale sky shrinks.
an ash-tray is slowly filling.

the old man with no fingers remembers
the shriek of the circular saw;

his belligerent jumper straining at the seams,
a leaking prostate dampening his spirits.

he had once had a trial with blackburn rovers.
he is dying of something he cannot spell.

seeing red

wozzabollocks!

ref ! ref man !
wozzafuck off-side !

thaz nee way a'm off-side there ref !
a'woz still in wor half when ee played the fuckin' baal !
an' that fat rightback woz stannin' on the penalty spot !
ee had t'be playin iz on ref ? y'mustivseen that ?
steviefuckinwonder cuddaseen that !

hat d'yi mean man? how cannabee off-side if a'm in me own poxy half ?
owcanna! howcanna? a'm here, he's there, ritchie knocks the baal ower
n' a've just done 'im for pace. tha's nee way a'm off-side !

zin man, a cudn't give a toss what the linesman did,
e's one o'their fuckin subs ! it's obvious what he's deein !

ah aye, that's right, fuckin book iz !
nat's jist fuckin typical that !
um fucker meks a stand against injustice
n' the fuckin repressive state apparatus
orings into fuckin action !

am calmed down man !

ey ref, a've seen some shite decisions like, but this takes the fuckin' biscuit !

e gan on, yi might as well fuckin send iz off

yi knaa what it is ref ?
woz brought up to have a profound dislike
r authoritarian types in black uniforms,
jist for once.... jist for fuckin once !
wud'a made a pleasant change t'have
formative years stereotype exploded
n a nice Saturday afternoon !
ut oh no ! you have to go an' fuckin blow it !

ignorant little wank !

e man ! aye ! I am fuckin going !

Rob Walton

'I grew up in a working-class family on a council estate in Scunthorpe, essentially a working-class town. As a child, I remember writing to the editor of the local paper expressing interest in becoming a journalist. I also recall winning a couple of little prizes in school for writing, so the interest was always there.

A year on the dole in London and Scunthorpe followed, before a move to study Creative Arts at what was then Newcastle Poly in the 1980s. I studied Drama and did a minor course in Creative Writing. Twenty years later I did a Creative Writing MA at Newcastle University.

Those two intervening decades were spent thinking I'd like to write and I'd like to be read. Sometimes I wrote things and sent them out. They came back.

I was lucky enough to have Jackie Kay as my personal tutor on my course, and she was both insightful and encouraging, but I still didn't think I belonged. Sessions by one tutor left me completely baffled. I didn't know what they were about or who they were for. I just knew it wasn't me.

It's only in the last few years I've realised I can write about what I want in the way I want. I didn't have any of that confidence before, and I think a lot of it can be put down to class. I'd had books, love and encouragement as a child, but didn't have the nous, the exposure, the contacts to get on. Setbacks were things that set me back. They didn't encourage me to persevere and overcome. I had no writing community.

Today I still feel like an outsider in many writing communities but, in my 50's, I can see that as a positive as well as a negative. I write about everyday experiences in everyday language, but there are some gatekeepers who prefer more cerebral and, frankly, more inaccessible writing. That's not what I do, and eventually—a long way down the line—I realise I don't have to, because there are many more avenues in print and online for a voice like mine to be heard.

Now I've had more work published and my name on the spine of a book, I feel the need to ensure I look around to see others who might need a helping hand, or a place to direct a fist.'

this industrial unit comes up to me

it's the lack of romance
in the needlessly printed ticket
because no-one's checking anything
at the gig in the former east end industrial unit
turned into a current east end industrial unit
only back in the day industrial units
didn't hold so many gigs
well at least not active and functioning
industrial units
and they weren't called industrial units
and I wonder if tonight's singing bloke
will have a song about industrial units
and how there used to be that industry thing
happening in them
and now there's that
thing where they might be making
needless pleasantries half the time
and coolness and image the other half
and you can probably get some industrial unit mementoes
on the industrial unit merch table

a new castle

It's early days but I've been
to the council's planning portal
and submitted my application
to build a new castle
away from the hustle
and bustle and commerce of the city centre

and we're going to use Throckley bricks
and the great feature
the u s bloody p
will be the gateway
which will weirdly be bigger than the rest
of the castle put together

and it will be big enough for everyone
yes everyone who wants to get in
can get in without ID or passes or lanyards
and the only stipulation is when they get in
they take it all apart
and help to build something a bit less castley

edges

may we all take our own sandwiches to the cinema
and take turns to proffer the popcorn

may the organ grinder and the knife sharpener
help carve all our names in a heart in a London plane

may there please be a moratorium
on more gin bars please

may the library open on Sundays for librarians
to waft ill-fitting words out of the windows

may people spill gracefully
from pubs selling beer labelled beer

may laughter spill from cafes
with one type of coffee

may boarded-up windows
provide reading matter at bus stops

may bus drivers pull in next to each other to talk bollocks
while passengers smile at their reflections in the other bus

may arguments on rainy streets get resolved
after we've all intervened

may birds shit on a couple pissing in an alley
while workers reinstate rough edges

may the end go on being nigh

Mela

On the Town Moor,
a forgotten and remembered corner
of England's once and future green and pleasant,
there is food and there is drink
and there are craft activities.

The dignitary looks around, says,
That looks lovely! What are they making?
A difference.
Aah, right, yes, I see.
I was being sarcastic.
Aah, right, yes, I see.

John Dobson's Hidden Masterpiece

There's this building only I can see.

It's a club for workers and also for folk who don't fancy working
but might want to read and get a break
of six or seven on one of the snooker tables
which slide together and flip over to form a dance floor
and Richard Grainger built some steps to get you up there
and John Clayton checked the Health and Safety regs.

It's a clever trick but when you then push
the tables/floor to one side a swimming pool
and wrestling ring are revealed
and the prices aren't fancy there
nor at the bar which has a sewing machine
at one end and an inbuilt retro games console

with pale ale pumps and tea pots
and smoothie makers at the other
and holders for modern game handsets
and VR goggles and the things that will come after
VR goggles and the things that will come after them
which you can probably wear to see John Dobson's hidden masterpiece.

Mass Observation Project

On the side of a bus
there's an ad for a film
that came out eight months ago.
Times are hard.

On the side of a bloke
there's a tattoo
of someone who left eight months ago.
Love is hard.

On the side of a building
there's some graffiti
about the goverment.
Spelling is hard.

On the side of a road
next to some graffiti
there's a tattooed bloke
waiting for a bus.
He's as soft as clarts.

tricks of the trade

there's a busker on northumberland street
holding a trumpet somewhere near his mouth
as the eye of the tiger backing track blares out
and maybe he once busked
in 42nd street or something
because he's only playing every 42nd note

Slippery

Mr Mosey
the council man
bided his time
and I pondered about him
being slow on the uptake before
e v e n t u a l l y
receiving a reply by snail mail
wherein he apologised
possibly sincerely and
certainly at length
and in great detail
about the reasons for the
slowness of the slide
in the so-called
adventure playground.
Central government had put the brakes on
public spending
and after due and diligent deliberation
delays had ensued with regard
to accelerated downward progress
on said slide

and he apologised for my child's
i n t e r m i n a b l e
wait for a soaking
in the terminus puddle
and if I could just
bear with them
the matter would be put to bed
in due course and in the meantime
the highways department
had some spare paint
which they would use
to create *go faster* stripes
on aforementioned slide
to give the illusion of speed
for the sons and daughters
of this fine city.

over the bridge

to save money on parking
and to keep some semblance of fitness
when I go to the cinema
but mostly to save money on parking
I leave the supposedly electric blue Zafira 1.6
next to the Cumberland Arms
and walk past the Polish bakery/shop
and then over Byker Bridge
where me and my daughter
did some supremely unsuccessful geocaching
nearly getting knocked over by a lovely young lad/
drug-crazed cyclo-nightmare zombie
on a bike I couldn't hear
and I feel slightly alarmed by the hurtling traffic

but I walk on with the interest
on my current account
growing all the time
and I go over the rotting staircase
which will most definitely collapse the next time
I use it and over the blue carpet
which is the least blue thing
anyone has ever seen
and then I get to the cinema
having missed the first twenty minutes of the film
but it doesn't matter
it's only twenty minutes
and I don't know if you heard
but I saved money on parking
yes I saved money on parking

That pizza place in the Grainger Market

A group of students are deciding on their slices
grinds of pepper
shakes of chilli flakes.

It gets busier.

A woman in an electric wheelchair
picks up a top at the clothes place opposite.
Behind her, her daughter texts.

I consider replacing my watch strap for £4.99
but then remember I replaced it yesterday
and I've only got so many wrists
and so many watch faces
and so much cash

and I'm all for supporting local businesses
but.

Also, I don't want to get hung up
on, like, the hours and the minutes, man.
So I shall let my new strap disintegrate
and tell the time by how many slices
of mixed veg pizza are left
or how many tops remain on the rail
and soon everyone will be using a nylon blousometer
to count down to Margherita hour.

As though they watched

As though they watched
and misinterpreted
a public information film
from before they were born
the ballgirls and ballboys
proper wobbly from Bovril
spill out of St James'
wearing black capes

As though they watched
a Keep Britain Tidy film
from before they were born
the ballgirls and ballboys
roam the city centre streets
picking up pink gin bottles
and discarded energy drinks cans
returning crisp packets
to pedestrians
and putting dog crap
in people's pockets

As though they watched
an avant-garde film
from before they were born
the ballgirls and ballboys
run up and down
Northumberland Street
shouting about lost bets
lost loves
and lost lives

Acknowledgements

Keith Armstrong: Many of the poems appeared previously in *The Month of the Asparagus: Selected Poems by Keith Armstrong*, Ward Wood Publishing, London 2011. *Splinters: Poems by Keith Armstrong*, Hill Salad Books (Breviary Stuff Publications), London 2011.

Jane Burn: 'Wave at Aeroplanes' was commended in the 2015 Yorkmix Poetry Competition. 'Are you still walking' first published in *Fresh Air Poetry*. Thistlecrack first published in *Crannog*.

Nev Clay: Some of the poems appeared in *The Leaf Collector*, Sand Publishing and the Maple Street press pamphlet *Small words from the great pause*.

Dan Douglas: the photographs are from the 2017 short film *bunstop*. Dan is a Tynemouth-based photographer and film maker. He and Paul Summers have collaborated on multiple projects over the years, from children's books to poetry films, together winning multiple awards for their work. More of Dan's work can be found at www.dandouglas.org

Catherine Graham: 'A Protest March', 'Factory Outing', 'Shift', 'Head of A Young Man In A Cap' and 'Putting Aunt Adeline On the Train' are from Catherine's Lowry-inspired pamphlet *Like A Fish Out Of Batter* (Indigo Dreams Publishing). 'I Beg To Apply For The Post' and 'Daughters of Tyne' are from Catherine's collection *Things I Will Put In My Mother's Pocket*, also Indigo Dreams Publishing. 'I Beg To Apply For The Post' was also previously published online at *The Recusant* (www.therecusant.org.uk) and *Proletarian Poetry* (www.proletarianpoetry.com). 'My Father Never Got Over Being Voted Off the Allotment' was previously published in the **Culture Matters** Bread and Roses Poetry Award anthology *We Will Be Free*.

Dan Johnston: Some of the poems first appeared in *An Overtaking and The Daredevil: Scenes from a Bigamist Marriage*, both Red Squirrel Press.

Kathleen Kenny: 'Playground of the Sacred Heart' is based on a traditional children's skipping song, 'The Wind Blows High'.

Lisa Matthews: Poems previously appeared in *Callisto*, Red Squirrel Press

Paul Summers: 'bunstop', from the filmpoem of same name, collaboration with Dan Douglas & Roma Yagnik. all other poems appeared in *last bus*, iron press 1998 / *union, new & selected poems*, Smokestack Books, 2011.

Rob Walton: edges was previously published in *It All Radiates Outwards* by Verve Poetry Press.